The FAMILY Who Loved Me

Written and Illustrated by

Pam Brown

The Family Who Loved Me

Pam Brown

The FAMILY Who Loved Me

PAGE PUBLISHING
Conneaut Lake, PA

First originally published by Page Publishing 2023

ISBN 979-8-88793-047-3 (pbk)
ISBN 979-8-88793-056-5 (hc)
ISBN 979-8-88793-052-7 (digital)

Printed in the United States of America

I remember the day like it was yesterday, but it was many years ago. I was feeling a bit sad and worn out. It was an ordinary day for a small home on Rodeo Lane. That's me.

Only the young boy named Bobby was home that day. He was about ten years old and lived with me along with his mom, dad, and older sister. But everyone else was gone that day. There was a knock on my door, so Bobby opened it. A new family had come to visit along with another lady.

Bobby asked them in because they wanted to see me. The new family had a mom, a dad, a little girl, and a little boy. They seemed very nice. Bobby told them right away about the fleas that were inside, and I know they saw the stains on my carpet. I felt a little embarrassed, but they tried to not notice how dirty and worn out I was.

They looked around every room, and they went outside. My yard was mostly weeds, and it had a small shed and a patio, not too much to see. The new family talked to the lady, and then they left. I felt kind of sorry to see them go. They seemed so nice, but I could see why they wouldn't want to stay.

Several weeks went by, and my life on Rodeo Lane stayed pretty much the same. No one seemed to notice or pay attention to me. I often thought about that family and wished they would visit again.

Then one day, things changed. The family that lived with me started packing. It didn't take long, and then it was so quiet. I was alone for several days. I was worried it would always be that way.

Not too long after that, I woke up one morning to the sound of cars pulling into my driveway. Then I heard voices; some grown-ups and some little children. That nice family had returned!

Over the next several days and weeks, the family settled in. They swept, cleaned, and polished as they brought in all of their belongings. I got to know my new family. I learned that the little girl was Kimberly and the little boy was Cameron. They seemed so happy to be moving in. It made me happy too.

I could tell my new family loved me. They took good care of me. They even painted me a bright blue!

They cut down all the weeds and planted grass and flowers. They planted a garden with tomatoes, pumpkins, and corn.

They even planted three small redwood trees. What a big surprise!

One day, they put in a cement walkway leading to the front door. While the cement was still wet, Kimberly and Cameron found a spot where they could put their handprints and write their initials. They were very small handprints since Kimberly was only four and Cameron was just three. They could always look at those small prints and remember that day.

Then one evening, my family came home with a new friend for me. They called her Pepper. She was a border collie, and she was full of energy.

She ran and ran all over my yard. She would even play soccer with Kimberly and Cameron. I loved listening to them laugh and play.

The years went by. We were all happy even though I was a very small house. There were many holiday parties.

Fourth of July was always a big day on Rodeo Lane. I was always decorated in red, white, and blue ribbons and flags. So many friends came to visit and to celebrate. There would be a big parade held right in front of me! The children in the neighborhood would march right passed me with their bikes and wagons all decorated.

Later, everyone would lay on my lawn and stare at the sky while fireworks burst above them.

There were other fun holidays too. Halloween and Christmas were two of my favorites. I would always get decorated every year. I loved when kids would knock on my front door on Halloween night so that we could give them candy.

And at Christmas, I would just sparkle with lights.

Then the building began. It started with a treehouse. I had a really big tree in my backyard, and Dad designed a fun tree house for the kids to play in. There were stairs that led up to a slide and a ladder that led up inside the tree house. The kids spent many hours with their friends playing in that tree. They even taught Pepper how to go up the stairs and down the slide.

Not too long after that, the big building began. Old walls came down, and new walls went up. I had always been a little home, but I was sure growing! So many new rooms were added. I got taller because now I had a second floor and so many windows! Now I could really see what was going on in my neighborhood. Everything was made shiny and new.

My new family liked to invite people over, which I really enjoyed. They would show their friends all the new things they had done to fix me up. I must admit, it made me feel so happy and proud.

My family liked to play lots of games, which made everyone laugh. My favorite game was hide-and-seek because I got to play along. While Mom would run and hide, Dad would hold on to Pepper. Then after I helped Mom hide really well, he would let Pepper go. Pepper would run up and down the stairs peeking in and out of rooms while Mom stayed so quiet. Pepper always found her though, and when she did, she would bark and bark and wiggle around because she was so excited.

Things went on happily for several years. The kids grew up, and it seemed like they weren't at home as much as they used to be. But we still had lots of good times.

Then one day, Kimberly was in her room packing. I had overheard them all talking about how Kimberly would be moving away to go to a place called college, a school for big kids. It seemed like everyone was excited and a little sad at the same time.

After she was gone, things got quieter. And then it wasn't too long before they started talking about Cameron moving away too. It would be so quiet without the kids here. It would just be Mom, Dad, Pepper, and me.

Another school year came and went when I heard that Cameron was coming home from college. I was so excited to have one of the kids home! I thought things would be like they used to be. But they weren't. Everyone was busy. I could hear Mom and Dad talking about plans, but I couldn't understand what that meant.

One day, I looked out front and saw that there was a sign on my lawn. I had seen signs like that before on other lawns, and I knew that meant one family would move away, and a new family would move into the neighborhood.

My family was moving away. I didn't understand why, but I knew they loved me and that they were sorry to leave me behind. I loved them too, and I would miss them.

They found a nice family for me, but I was sad the day they packed the last of their things. I watched as they got in their cars, drove down the street, turned the corner, and then drove away.

About ten years after they moved away, there was a knock on my front door. My new family opened the door, and Kimberly was standing there. She had come back to visit me. She lived far away now but hadn't forgotten me.

My new family was happy to show Kimberly around. They wanted her to see the new things they had done and what was still the same. I could tell that Kimberly was happy when she looked down from my steps and saw the handprints that she and Cameron made in the cement when they were so little.

Kimberly also saw that the small redwood trees they had planted so long ago were now taller than my roof.

When it was time for Kimberly to go, she said goodbye and then drove away. I was sad to see her go. But I was thankful for her visit. I was also grateful for her family—the family who loved me.

about the Author

Pam Brown is a teacher, an artist, and an author. She now lives in Liberty, Utah, but was born and raised in California. She is married to Kyle and has two children, Kimberly and Cameron. She also has five wonderful grandchildren. Pam earned her bachelor of arts degree from BYU in Provo, Utah, and then went on to complete her teaching credential through California State, Hayward in California. She loves art, especially pastel painting, and has used that love of pastels to create the illustrations in her book.

She also loves to tell stories, so she has been able to combine both her love of art and storytelling into this story that is near and dear to her heart. Pam also loves to spend time outdoors hiking, biking, riding, gardening, and playing pickleball with friends. She has taught school for over thirty years. Pam enjoyed working art and storytelling into so many of her lessons over the years.

CPSIA information can be obtained
at www.ICGtesting.com
Printed in the USA
JSHW042150070623
42892JS00005B/54

9 798887 930473